in my head

Shanice Perez

BookLeaf Publishing
India | USA | UK

Presentation by *BookLeaf Publishing*

Web: www.bookleafpub.com

E-mail: info@bookleafpub.com

ISBN: 9789363319776

First edition 2024

ACKNOWLEDGEMENT

In the making of these series of poems there is many people through out my life that I want to acknowledge. My father for always supporting me and wanting the best for me. My mother for always being by my side. My grandma who I feel raised me and still is watching me grow. Ms. Candelaria for completing my circle, she always supported me and knows i can go beyond what I set for myself. Ms. Desai for helping my creative ability and pushing me forward. Ms. V for telling me to keep dreaming and not be afraid. My friends Ashley, Sammy and Cory for just always having my back and being my best friends in the whole world. My siblings Frida, Sebastian, and Xander for being the best siblings I could ever ask for, I hope we are siblings in every universe. My friend Victoria for also going on a writing journey with me and pushing me to get my work out into the universe. Lastly, you guys for just existing and appreciating my art.

PREFACE

I just want you to know someone out their understands how you must feel, connection.

behind the smile

Corrupted Angels,
Fall from the sky,
With their broken wings,
Left there to die.

When you meet her,
She's a pretty little thing,
When you know her,
Her demons are released.

So watch your back,
She might release her pain,
Wait,
She's close,
You might get sucked into her game.

But to only realize,
That broken girl's game,
Is one you must play,
To put her back together again.

The side others see

Words can bring me down,
But an action that hurts,
Can make me crumble,
Under your touch.

Some call me weak,
But wonder why I get back up,
With a smile.

Some call me strong,
But wonder why I stay blank,
With no emotion.

I prefer determined,
Because I know when I'm weak,
Turning the other cheek,
And that's why the others call me strong.

Known

Sometimes I feel that,
I hurt everyone around me.

I'm scared that,
The broken cannot be fixed.

To fix my problem,
I block who needs me most.

I don't want to be known as,
The crumbler.

I want to be known as,
The builder.

So that I can fix everyone,
That has ever been broken.

Loving you

I'll love you for eternity,
And eternity never ends,
But it hurts when you say,
"Let's just be friends."

I've loved you forever now,
But forever seems like such a short amount of
time,
When you love someone as much as,
I love you.

Gone

Around this time,
I wish I was gone.

Gone away,
With the wind,
Washed up on a shore,
Far away.

I keep running,
No longer can I keep up,
As they drag me back into the ocean.

Waves crash,
Emotions mashed,
I don't know what to feel.

Years later,
I still wish I was gone,
The pain is catching up with me.

Dripped on the pages,
Water from the ocean like tears on my face,
The salt burns my eyes,
It won't go away.

I wish I was gone.

Turn it off

Pitter patter of the rain,
Playing through the speakers,
Turn it off.

The blue light on a dark screen,
Bright enough to leak through my lids,
Turn it off.

Covered in blankets,
Comfortable but not comforting,
Turn it off.

Lying restless and awake,
Left with a dry throat from the air,
Turn it off.

Thoughts run through my brain like a marathon,
Thinking of everything yet nothing comes to
mind,
Please just turn it off.

Stop yelling at me

I know what I did was wrong,
I was just a kid,
Stop yelling at me.

I know I have a lot of growing up to do,
I need to be left alone,
Stop yelling at me.

I know I need to be a good example,
It's the weight on my shoulders,
Stop yelling at me.

I know you don't like how I dress,
I don't know how else to express myself,
Stop yelling at me.

I know I am lazy,
I'm just too tired to do anything,
Stop yelling at me.

I know you aren't yelling at me,
I want you to stop telling me how to live,
Just let me figure it out,
So please,
Stop yelling at me.

Exhausted

A sigh,
Almost like a breeze of exhaustion.

A slouch,
Tired of carrying problems on my shoulders.

A face with no emotion,
Not wanting to waste the energy to pretend.

Being the oldest wasn't easy,
No one asked to take this position yet it was
given,
I'm so exhausted.

Brother

courAgeous as a Lion,
as restless as a lEaf in the wind,
warm like a Xenial host offering greetings,
an embrAce of kiNdness and reliability,
Dextrous and dEbonair,
skillful yet chaRming,
my lovely brother,
ALEXANDER.

Twins

Twins,
The flames joined with no separation,
Growing apart as they differ.

Twins,
One like a tea kettle,
Short and stout,
the other like a tree,
Sturdy and indifferent.

Twins,
Tea kettles whistle,
A spirit of Determination,
Trees absorb your worries,
Vigorous growth.

A pea can roll out of its pod,
Together they were born,
Beautiful to each their own,
Twins.

My North Stars

The one who started this group,
The one who followed through,
The one who sees us every night,
The one who won't go down without a fight,
The one who stresses out alone,
The one who is always on his phone,
The one who had a surge of confidence,
The one who films the moments,
The one who manages behind the scenes,
Because of you,
Your stars shine through,
And because of your stars,
You light up the dark.

rain

Drip Drop.

The rain spoke.

Drip Drop.

The rain cried.

Drip Drop.

The sky fell.

Drip Drop.

So did I.

Drip Drop.

mask

Look closely,
I'm a person of many,
The feeling describes me,
My smile covers my hurting heart,
My eyes cry many tears,
Behind my laugh, I'm falling apart,
But look closely,
You will see,
The girl smiling is not me.

Rehab

I sat in my cell alone for the most part,
Trapped in a room,
Where it's me, myself, and I,
What did I do to deserve this,
I'm trapped within my bounds,
You say in getting better,
But oh what a lie,
I can seem to remember who you are,
Or who am I,
To me you're just another faceless beauty,
But you will never understand,
You are my rehab.

Cherish

Think about it,
Everything you have,
Could be taken away within minutes,
On a sunny day everyone's happy,
Could be automatically changed.

A sun to lights out,
A smile to a thousand tears,
Make sure to love what you have,
Before it disappears.

Matter

The matter of the stars,
Is not the same as in our hearts,
Atoms break and so do hearts.

A fragment of a second makes up a year,
However within myself,
I am lost,
I am matter.

Hypocrite

Look upon me,
Only you see through me,
Never have I been so isolated,
Evermore will I be so faded,
Lastly, you see me,
I smell of guilt and remorse,
Never been similar to a corpse,
Eager to say goodbye,
Severity in all that dies,
Slowly slipping into your white lies.

To be

Be kind,
To yourself and others.

Be free,
Unlock the chains that hold you down.

Be light,
Take the weight off your shoulders and fly.

Be wise,
Use your knowledge to help others.

Don't be burdened by your role,
You'll realize it once you let go,
Be the best you can be,
Then you'll see,
It's not so bad,
To be me.

Friends

Near and far,
Across the globe to next door,
You'll be there.

So many but so little,
Not as frequent as the bus I take,
Stop dawn to late.

Time plays tricks,
It's hard to communicate,
Even when not spoken to,
We pick back up like yesterday's date.

From me to you,
Happy or blue,
I'm glad you are here for me,
No matter where you are,
My friends.

3

Three pebbles,
I hold it in my palm.

Cherished,
Three roses in my garden.

Watching over me,
Soaring like three birds in the sky.

Beautiful, Tough, and Free,
I love my three.

peace

a time when the wars stop,
a time when people can stay true,
a time when we protect what has been given,
that's when there will be peace.

peace of mind,
to walk down the street and not fear for life,
to have clear waters and skies,
to not have man-made food and dyes.

take away the chemicals,
take away the plastics and waste,
take away violence and crime,
that's when there will be peace,
peace of mind.